To Mirte and Seppe,
who make me rediscover the world every single day.
— Jan Leyssens

IS THERE LIFE IN OUTER SPACE?

Written by Jan Leyssens
Illustrated by Joachim Sneyers

Clavis
NEW YORK

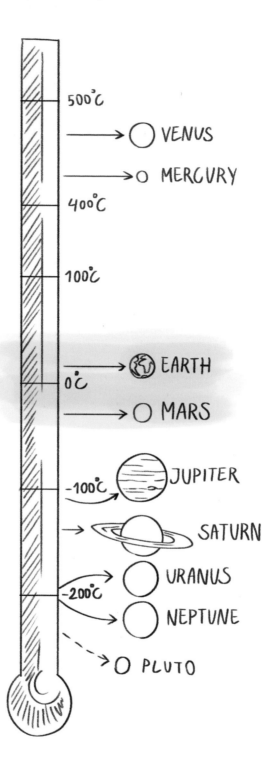

E arth is a wonderful planet. It's just far enough from the sun to get not *too* hot and just close enough to be not *too* cold. And do you know how many grains of sand there are on our earth? Well, the universe has almost as many stars as the tiny grains here on earth! Within that huge group of stars, astrobiologists look for planets that resemble ours, and where other life might be possible.

In the early 1800s, most people were convinced that the moon, Mars, and Venus were inhabited. Scientists wrote stories about how they had seen cities on the moon and canals on Mars with their telescopes. They believed creatures lived there, but we could not reach them. The Austrian astronomer Joseph Johann von Littrow suggested digging out large canals and ditches in the Sahara Desert that could be filled with oil and then set on fire, using earth as if it were a gigantic drawing board to send messages to Mars at night.

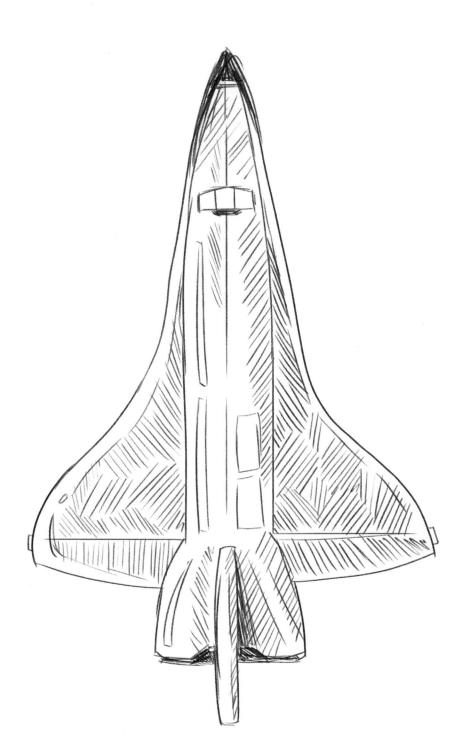

By now we know that there's no life on the moon. Mars may have been livable at one time, but the planet's water is now frozen under rocks. Using better telescopes that can look deeper into space, we discovered that there are quite a few Earth-like planets. However, they're so far removed from our planet that we're not able to go there. As a result, the same question from two hundred years ago remains: if extraterrestrial life exists, how can we contact them, so they know that we also exist?

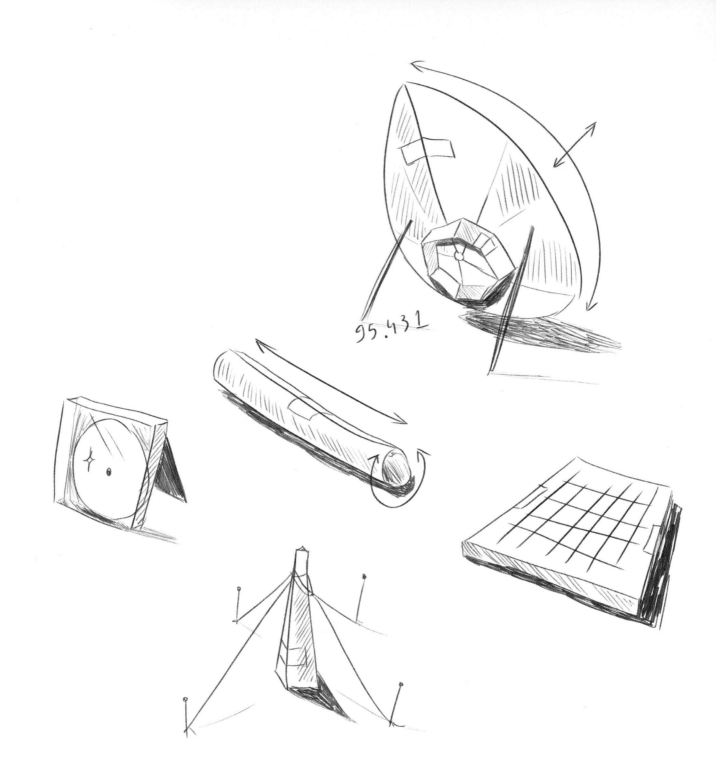

95.432

Carl Sagan was an astrobiologist who was always looking for ways to contact extraterrestrial life. Then Carl heard about the two satellites of NASA's Voyager program. After the satellites had traveled around the farthest planets in our solar system—Jupiter, Uranus, Neptune, and Pluto—they would fly outside our solar system. It was the first time hand-made objects could do such a thing. For Carl, it was the perfect opportunity to give a message to extraterrestrials.

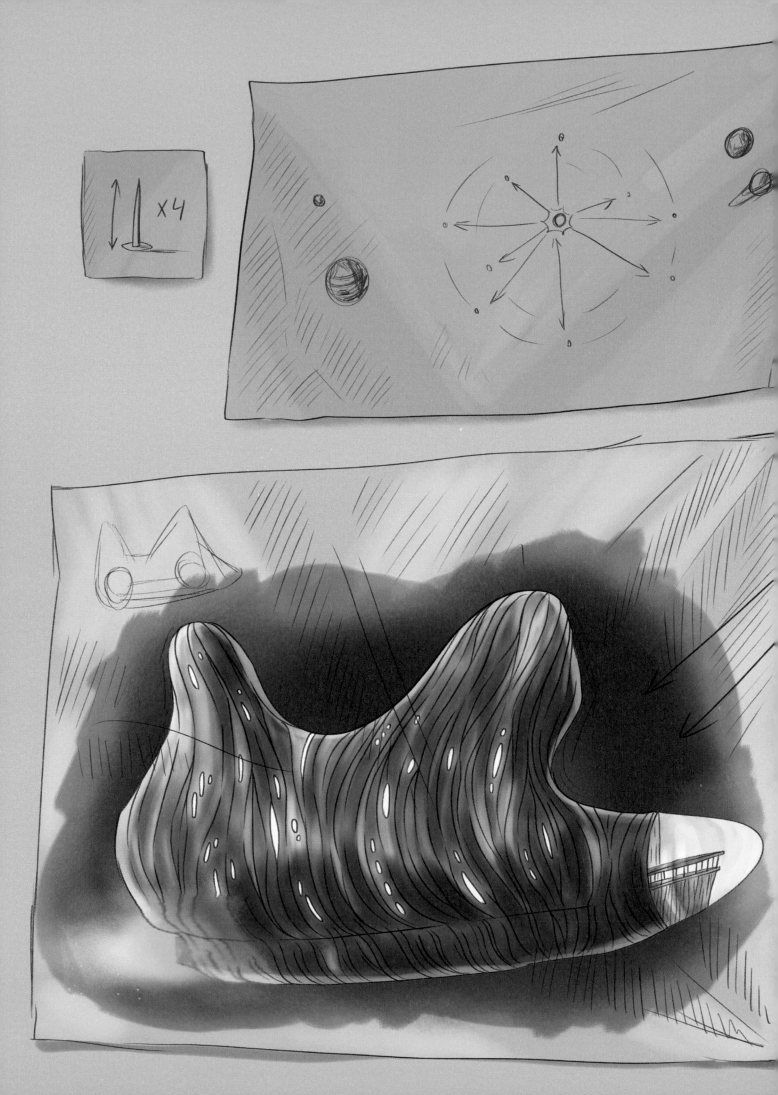

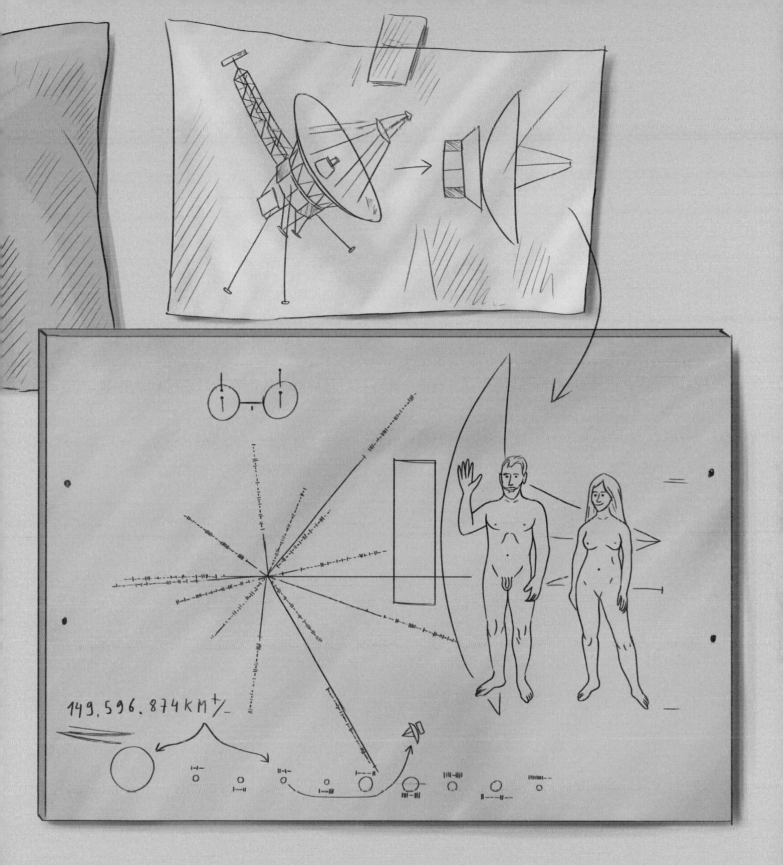

In 1972, five years before the Voyager program, Carl, Frank Drake, and Linda Salzman worked together to design golden plaques that were attached to the Pioneer 10 and Pioneer 11 satellites. The plaques featured drawings of a man and a woman, as well as the locations of the sun and our planet in the galaxy. However, for the Voyager missions, Carl wanted to provide more than just a small drawing. But how would he do it?

Carl came up with the idea of sending sounds and images into space along with a drawing similar to that of the Pioneer satellites. The golden plaque then became a golden record—like a CD but bigger. If the extraterrestrials followed the instructions correctly, they would hear sounds from the Earth and even discover images.

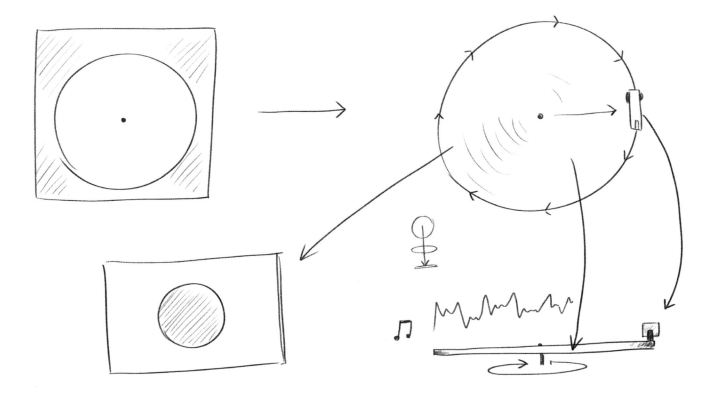

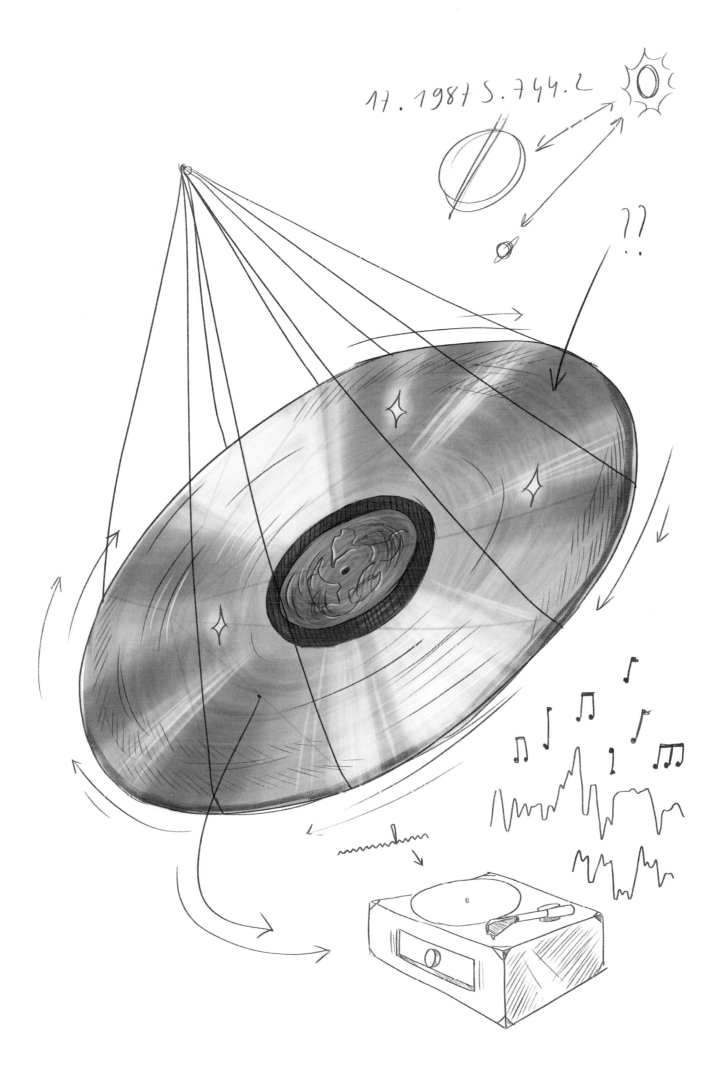

Carl organized a group of astrobiologists to develop the idea. What should he put on such a record? What does the earth sound like? The record could be played on two sides, with space for about a hundred images and a maximum of two hours of sound. Which pictures and sounds best describe earth?

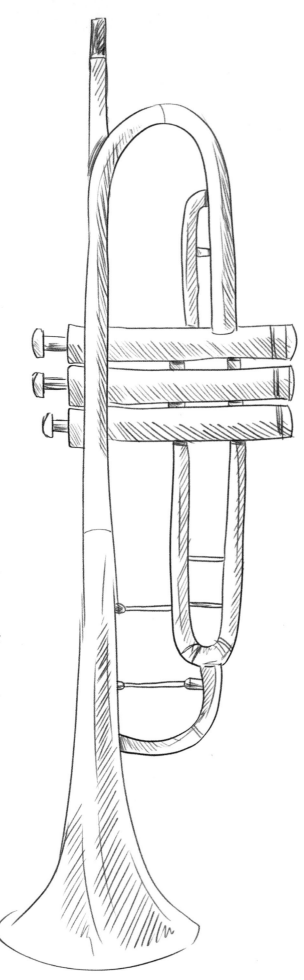

They collected images and sounds from all over the world. It took the group a year to decide which ones to include in the mission. Eventually, they decided to send 115 pictures of people, handmade things, and nature. For the sounds, they chose 55 greetings in different languages, music from all over the world, as well as human sounds, such as laughter and footsteps.

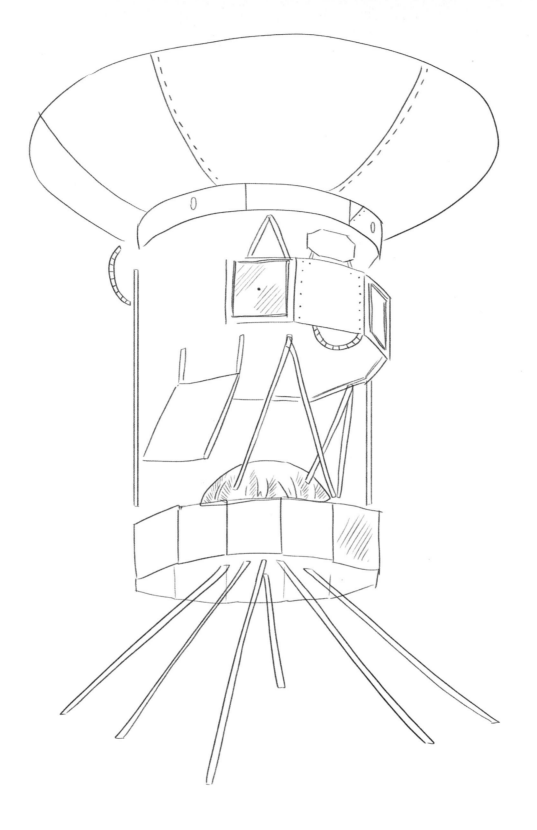

The Voyager satellites were launched in 1977. Carl's golden record with the drawing was attached to the satellites in search of extraterrestrial life. Carl compared this to a bottle being launched into the cosmic ocean. He saw the record as more than just a message for aliens. It was also a way to make people around the world think about what humans have and what we can do.

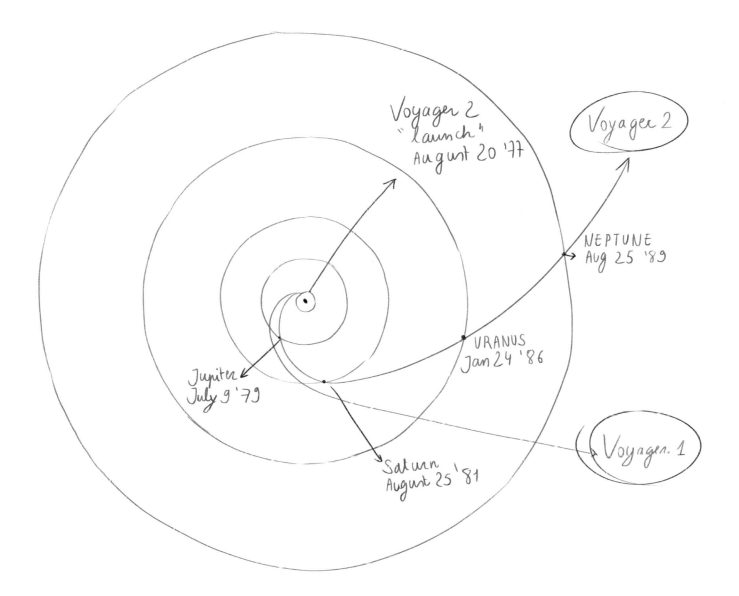

The original mission of the Voyagers was completed in 1989, but it was soon extended to investigate the outer edges of our solar system. The satellites showed fantastic images of the planets, but they also indicated that some of the moons around Jupiter might be inhabitable for humans. On August 25, 2012, Voyager 1 was the first hand-made object ever to leave our solar system. Six years later, Voyager 2 did the same.

NASA predicts that we can make contact with the Voyager satellites until at least 2025. Then, the satellites will be too far away to reach them. However, as long as they fly around, they keep sending messages into space. Eventually, we may get an answer from other extraterrestrial life. Until that happens, the work continues for those who want to discover more about space. In February 2019, NASA announced that they were going to send a team of astronauts to the moon again. This time, the goal is to live there.

95.43"